I0474443

© Copyright 2020

Title: Lady Leader

Author: Krusha Patel

© 2020, Krusha Patel

Self-publishing

To everyone in my support network,

and for my parents

Table of Contents

Acknowledgements

Last year I wrote my first book INFJ: How to be happy, feeling misunderstood. My inspiration came from, my previous role, where I suffered severe depression, anxiety and post-traumatic stress, then in July 2018 and was signed off work. It was a challenging period of my life. Years of my childhood in school were consumed with bullying, being told I was fat, useless or for bullying for being a teacher's pet. Many of my teachers knew I was good student with an instable thirst for knowledge and to learn and progress.

Since then to now I have been on a journey back to discovering myself. Throughout my journey my parents have supported me all the way. They have watched all my ups and down, seen me at my worst, and praised me at my best. Without their support and nurturing I wouldn't have been able to publish my first book and continue to help others with this book.

My sincere thanks to everyone who has helped me through my life, seen my struggles, my business adventures, career changes and those who encouraged me to write. You have offered me endless support.

LADY LEADER

About the Author

Krusha Patel started her journey into becoming an author when she suffered from several metal health issues. She reached a turning point in her life where she left her position, working as a management accountant within the finance industry. She then transitioned into a more fulfilling role based on her experience as a qualified site supervisor, to helping and assisting project managers and contractors within the construction industry.

Though her experience and self-journey through mental illness, she authored her first book INFJ: How to feel happy, feeling misunderstood. Her first book was inspired by her own journey through suffering through severe depression, anxiety, PTSD (post dramatic stress disorder) and suicidal thoughts.

Krusha is a business and personal coach with experience and knowledge in NLP. Krusha has helped several private business coaching clients to grow their business and helped her personal coaching clients, with personal issues. Krusha is also a business owner having her own accounting and consultancy practice as well as an investment company, she is also a qualified mental health first aider. She is continually inspired by the feedback she has received, in how she has helped others. She has met with influential businessmen and actors some of which include John Lee, Vincent Wong, Armand Morin.

Introduction

Communication not only constitutes one of the crucial aspects of leadership performance, but leadership can productively be viewed as a communication process. Humour is one of the prime means which enables leaders to achieve their various transactional as well as relational objectives. This book aims at exploring one of the ways in which women leaders make use of this particularly versatile discursive strategy in order to enhance their leadership performance while also resolving the challenges of being the `left out' in a predominantly masculine work environment.

The construction industry plays very significant role in the development of every country in terms of infrastructural and promoting investment. The industry is however, seen as a preserve of men. It is against this backdrop, that women's participation in the industry was assessed. We will look at specific roles of women, their representation in construction industry, whether women are adequately engaged in management position and their challenges in terms of different levels of motivations in the industry.

Many women are deterred from participation or feel that it is overwhelming to have a job particularly in male-dominated industries, because of the lack of family role models, stereotypes about the nature of 'women's work.' Some workplaces even discouraging cultures and structural problems within those organisations.

Around the world, the underrepresentation of women in industries considered to be 'male-dominated', continues to affect gender equality, industry performance and our nation's economy even though in the most recent years this has improved vastly. By 'maledominated', I am referring to industries such as mining, utilities and construction. Women only account for 12% of professional working roles in construction, within the United Kingdom, this statistic is taken from the government's website as at July 2019.

However, a number of leaders in male-dominated industries, in the United Kingdom and overseas, have recognised the underutilised pool of talent that women represent. They have taken commendable and highly effective steps to change their organsational cultures in ways that both attract female employees and help them to thrive. This is has come to light more in the last 3 to 5 years than it has been in the past. This is not about special treatment for women, but about the implementation of integrated gender diversity strategies, as well as how women can best show their true potential.

Have you ever felt as though you should leave a workplace, due to sexism? This book has been developed as a resource that is structured to encourage continued discussion and engagement on strategies to increase women's recruitment and retention in male-dominated industries.

Do you feel heard in your current workplace? Do you have suggestions for improvements that you have not voiced, or have not been heard? Women should be encouraged to share their views on what strategies are working or not, and what new strategies are being developed within any workplace.

According to CNBC, some of the most heavily male occupations or industuries revolve around an ambulance drivers and attendants, personal financial advisors, web developers, paramedics, biomedical and agricultural engineers, security analysts and this in construction and brick masonary. These are still all steadily increasing.

Women should be encouraged to take on responsibility to develop and expand into leadership roles within organisations. They should have access to develop and implement constructive and sustainable strategies to increase the representation of women in non-traditional roles especially in male-dominated industries.

Chapter 1

What's Stopping Women Achieving Their Potential

Helping women achieve their full potential is one of the most powerful ways to fight discrimination. Women continue to face tremendous barriers to success, even in the modern world, some of these still include the gender pay gap. Some women often find they have limited access to the productive resources like land, finance, and information that they need to grow their businesses. If we look at women, they are generally more so victims to violence, sexisim and discrimination. In most cases, women juggle the bulk of household, childcare responsibilities and place a concerted effort to improve their skills and earn independent incomes.

Most women I have come across have mentioned that the bulk of their concerns face towards family anf raising their children, as well as making sure that household is managed. This leads to the more sterotypical role of a women within society. The question we should be asking is are we empoering our younger generation enough to non-conform to sterotypes? Yes most women like to get married and have children, however there are so many ambitious women out there who want to have a business, be self suffient and financially stable in themselves. Are you one of them?

It's my belief that investing in opportunities for women could have tremendous economic and social impact. If women had the same access as men to training, information, and resources, they could increase productivity in most organisations, women are also known to be effective communicaters hence would be good at monitoring communication channels and stakeholder enagement. And on a wider scale, a recent study estimated that women's equal participation in the labour market would increase the global GDP by 26%, or $28 trillion. Women's economic empowerment not only promotes greater economic development but greater equity, opportunity, and social progress.

Women around the world continue to face systemic barriers and frustrations in the workplace. While this is a universal issue, the details differ from country to country, shaped by cultural and economic forces. According to a recent survey of business students and alumni conducted by the Global Network for Advanced Management, "Women remain underrepresented in business leadership roles worldwide, and intriguing variation across the globe and even across industries within the same country suggests that there is more to blame than culture of patriarchy."

From some interviews and roundtables with employees in the mining, construction and utilities industries it has been highlighted that some barriers. These are likely to have historical roots and are still apparent today. There should be addressed to increase women's representation.

These barriers include:

- **Lack of family role models:** From the very start, women are not exposed to career paths in the mining, construction and utilities industries as early or as often as men. Many men learn about potential roles in these industries from their fathers or other male relatives. However, women are not likely to come across these opportunities until later in life especially if they do not have access to male role models in these industries.

- **Negative perception and lack of awareness:** Even with the 'right' education, relatively few women are choosing to consider and apply for roles within male-dominated industries. Part of the reason is a negative or limited perception of the industries or anecdotal feedback from others about their negative experiences. Another factor is a lack of awareness of the opportunities and the career paths that are available to women within these industries.

- **Stereotypes and myths about women in the workplace:** Organisations within these male dominated industries are not addressing the stereotypes and assumptions about the sort of work women can do. Women can often develop or possess the skills to do the job. Often it is sterotypes that women are not aware of their potential performance and their commitment to their careers.

These stereotypes and myths about a womans' lack of ability and aspiration affects the roles women women would consider for a career path. They often are percieved based on what society thinks they should do (such as caring and motherhood) are then used to justify the activities of organisations that exclude women from recruitment and development activities.

- **Workplace culture:** Male-dominated industries are perceived to have a masculine or 'blokey' culture that is non-inclusive and has a higher tolerance of behaviors that could be viewed as sexual harassment, bullying, and discrimination. This leads to a perception that jobs within these organisations would be a challenge at every stage of a career, not just at senior leadership. Some perceptions include the presumption that women also need to adopt a 'blokey' personality to fit in within this industry.

- **Perception of (and actual) gender specific bias:** These industries are perceived to have a bias against women in relation to recruitment, development and career advancement, particularly in roles that are nontraditional and at the senior leadership level. This perception is then reinforced by the low percentages of women that work in these industries. In some industries women are also faced with with overlooked for progression against their male counterparts who are consequently promoted.

- **Structural issues:** These industries, particularly mining, have a culture of long hours and many don't offer flexibility and work-life balance, especially with women focusing on more than their career. This is particularly true for roles where workers need to fly in to remote locations. There is also a perception that organisations in these industries fail to offer workplace facilities and uniforms that are inclusive of women. Some organisations even go to the point of discrimitating female candidates who are pregnant due to time off for maternity leave.

How to achieve your professional potential as a woman

60% of European graduates are women and they make up 50% of the workplace. Although the number of women on boards in the U.K. is increasing, the gender wage gap stays at 20%. Here are top 10 tips that is highly recommend after coaching thousands of women to reach their professional potential.

1. Know yourself

Spending time identifying your strengths, development needs, success stories and transferable skills is important to creating a solid strategy to manage and develop your career. As an exercise take one piece of paper and draw a line down the middle, on one side write all your current strengths and of the other side all your weaknesses.

This will better help you to see the aspects of your job or personality that don't match your current strengths or play more to your weaknesses. For example, if your weakness is being able to handle conflict, then as a receptionist or first point for any issues it will be difficult to handle this type of role for work. Take time to assess your current position of work.

Also take a separate list of transferrable skills. On a separate piece of paper write down a list of skills you have or utilise at present. Find the jobs or position that you wish to have and then compare your skills that you can use in this role to approach it at an angle to use it towards your favour. This is key especially when applying or considering roles that lead to promotion and career development. Take note of what each role is looking for and if you have the current skills applicable to that role.

2. Have goals

A study released last year by Citi Group and LinkedIn indicated that women and men measure success in different ways. However, it is important for women to have an idea of their goals, write them down and communicate them to the people who need to know, particularly their boss, and partner. Women often feel embarrased to speak about their goals to be promoted within the workpace, at times not even knowing how to ask for a promotion or increase in wage.

Many women don't have clarity on their ambitions and get passed over. If you do not know where you are headed, every path is potentially right (or wrong). Many women find they are indeed ambitious but they do not put a price tag on their ambition in the way that men do. Many also lack focus in their careers as their focus lies mainly in family and nurturing.

A few tips for promotion within the workplace include having regular meetings and check up with your supervisor on how you are progressing and how you can be considered for promotional opportunities. Makes a list of the current work conducted and any additional work taken on, to view the progress and additional responsibilities. If you are also able to take on projects (big or small) and complete them successfully, this can be added to your portfolio for successes. In any case you will so need to find out what your current supervisors targets and milestones in order to help them and the company achieve them. This way if you keep track of the progress made you can develop a case where you are recognised for the work you have done, meeting up regular meetings will also help to keep you accountable in the workplace. Some organisations will also assist towards helping out employees that would like to be considered with additional qualification, speaking to your supervisor or relevant person in this case will show you are taking initiative and want to progress.

3. Create a strategy

"A goal without a plan, is just a wish."

It is important to create a plan to achieve your short-term goals, which are a stepping stone to your longer term vision. It might be to extend your network, learn a new skill or take on a new project. Some things do just fall into our laps, but mainly it all comes down to planning and preparation.

Many people have heart of SMART goals, if you have not, I suggest looking this up. This is when you will create goals that are specific, measurable, achievable, realistic and timed. For example, saying you want to lose weight or have more money, this can be achieved if a week. If you lose 1 lb you have lost weight and if you get £1 or $1 you have more money your goal is reached. However, if you set out a goal such as, I would like to lose 1 stone of weight by the 31st December 2020. You can look at this target and say it is specific, measurable in weight, achievable, realistic and dated by a specific time.

You then will need to further break this goal down into monthly, weekly and daily milestones. Having a diary to do this will also help. Look at your goals every day and have a look if I plan to lose 1 stone in a year, what do I need to achieve every month or every week. For example, to lose a stone (6.3kilos) in weight in a year I need to lose at least 1 kilo every 2 months. How will I do that, either you can set fitness goals, such as I need to cut out sugar and commit to working out 2 or 3 times a week for 30 minutes minimum. This breaks it down into achievable small steps.

4. Have a strong online professional presence

All women should have a strong online professional profile, to showcase your skills and achievements and establish professional visibility and credibility. LinkedIn at the present is the most common professional and career related social media platform. Make sure you have a good business photo (head and shoulders, no partners, children or animals) and check that your social media accounts have no inappropriate content or images and employers will sometimes look for this on social media as well.

5. Strengthen your network

Women tends to be multiplex networkers who network with people they know and trust. Try moving out of your comfort zone to extend your network to people that you may not know but who will be helpful career connections. You can also support these efforts via online contacts if you are a little bit nervous. Sometimes if you go to seminar and networking events especially in and around London or Europe your network and opportunities will grow.

6. Put your hand up

You will get left behind if you do not put your hand up and ask, whether it is for a new project or a pay rise. Women step up to negotiations six times less than men during their careers, this is to their detriment. With the gender pay gap sticking at 20%, it is necessary to understand your market value and position yourself accordingly. Maybe you need to ask for a mentor, professional training, a promotion or a stretch assignment. Do not wait for opportunities to come to you but be proactive instead.

7. Watch your language

By that I do not mean stop swearing – which I would recommend anyway, but rather not to fall into the sand traps that many women find themselves in. Use power words ('led,' 'achieved,' 'delivered'), stop apologising and asking permission. We do it all the time without even noticing. See if you can try to brand yourself if a way that you are seen to be a leader.

8. Body language and professional image

You never get a second chance to make a good first impression. Women are also judged more harshly in the recruitment and selection process by men on appearance. It is important to have good posture and eye contact as well as a strong professional image. Make sure you have a capsule professional wardrobe to project the right image for your dream job.

9. Invest in yourself

Many women prefer to spend money on a great looking handbag than invest in their professional development. Life-long learning is now a buzz workplace phrase but it is important to stay current in your field. There are many free or cheap online resources for continued learning. You can also ask your company to sponsor you. Taking a few career development or skills courses may help you to take charge within your career and development.

10. Become self-sufficient

Make sure that you are financially prepared for the unexpected or a crisis. We live in uncertain times and we never know what lies around the corner. Do not rely on your boss and your company to take care of your career, the life you live comes out the choices you make and your reaction to those choices and changes.

Empowering Women to Reach Their Full Potential

Imagine a world where society values every woman's informal and unpaid contributions and compensates her fairly for them. What would your status and income be? Wouldn't you be better positioned to pursue your dreams and realise your full potential?

For many women, in developed as well as developing countries, caregiving is the contribution that is largely informal and unpaid. As a result, on one end of the spectrum, you have women who are dropping out of their careers or going part-time in order to look after children or parents; on the other end, you have women who have no income, status or access to health care for themselves.

What's more, this caregiving work is on the rise due to longer life expectancies, which, on one hand is a sign of great scientific progress. On the other hand, this is placing more demands on caregivers with elderly family members. Though men have become more involved in family and household responsibilities, it is still primarily women who carry the majority of the health monitoring and care burdens for their families as well as their extended families and communities. To better empower women withing the work place the following three points should be considered.

• Value women by insuring development and implementation of policies that support women and enable them to integrate social, biological and occupational contributions. Gender-responsive social, economic, environmental and health policies should help women combine their varied roles and provide them with opportunities to advance their careers and leadership.

- Compensate women equally for formal and informal work. In one study, it is documented that 45–57% of women's work is unpaid (as compared to 24–44% of men's), and on average, women spend 2.3 hours per week on unpaid contributions. Since women have many informal roles, and 60% of all health care providers are informal workers (family members), we recommend making their work visible and developing strategies to insure pay balance/equity in pay, including benefits.

- Count women for better planning and for identifying discriminations and inequities. Sex desegregated data is essential for constructing comprehensive plans for women's health, work and leadership across the life course.

We can better establish mechanisms for insuring accountability to women that will protect the continuity and sustainability of the other three recommendations.

In the end, perhaps women's work should not be defined as employment, formal or informal, but in terms of the time and energy they expend in all activities, the relationships they foster, the personal and environmental resources they mobilize and the social and societal affirmation and valuation they do and do not receive. Adding these factors together are a more accurate depiction of women's work, which profoundly influences their health, and in turn, the health of their families and communities. We envision that these recommendations will empower women to reach their full potential in all aspects of their lives and in all of the roles they continuously integrate.

Chapter 2

Finding Strengths and Weaknesses

When seeking new opportunities, you may find yourself
wondering whether they will be fulfilled in a different industry or
position, and it turns out, that finding a career that makes you
happy can be a big challenge in itself. I went through this same
process. Understanding what your greatest strengths and
weaknesses are, can help you to learn more about yourself and
what you look for in a career.

Knowing certain traits about yourself also allows you to know
what to look out for in certain jobs and their working conditions,
so that you can be the happiest version of yourself in any position
you land. There are a few ways in which you can identify your
strengths, weaknesses, and everything in between.

1.   Take a break

More often than not, most people who are looking for a career
change based on what they're suited for, find themselves in a sea

of opportunities and will not be able to easily make up their mind when confronted with similar positions in different industries. They may be worn between locations, salaries, work requirements, working hours, etc. Grabbing the opportunity of having a long-weekend to focus is recommended. It could be just what you need to do to de-stress, have an open mind and start evaluating your strengths and weaknesses.

2.   Self-evaluation

Give yourself some time to think about the previous job that you may have had. Did you have sales and marketing jobs before? Perhaps in finance? Whether they were in the same industry or a range of others, you can still isolate the elements of what your job required and see which ones seemed most appealing to you.

- What did you enjoy most?
- What did you like least?
- When did you feel successful?
- When did you feel overwhelmingly stressed?

Asking yourself these questions may help you understand the way in which you like to work, for example, you may have just realised that although you can work in a team, you would much rather like to focus on your work by yourself, at your own pace, in your own space. In this case, you may find that you're not as motivated and proficient in your work when working with others. This is alright because there is a multitude of positions available that require individuals that would need to work mostly by themselves, just like there is a wide range of positions that require a number of team-players. These types of questions and answers will be able to give you an insight into what your strengths and weaknesses are, helping you achieve a sense of self-knowing.

3.   Qualifications and Experience

If you already know which direction you'd like to take your career to, the next step you should do is review your resume, where you will encounter one of three scenarios:

1. You have all the qualifications/experience necessary to take your next step

2. You have none of the qualifications/experience necessary to take your next step.

3. You're missing some of the qualifications/experience required

If you find yourself in one of the last two scenarios, there's no need to worry. Many times, the strength of your CV may be that you have been 10 years with the same company, showing that you are reliable, trustworthy and a long-term asset. Another scenario could be that you just graduated from University, without much experience in your specialty yet – your strength would be that you are young and have fresh ideas, ready to start working and learning in a junior position, however full of determination to grow into a senior position in a couple of years.

On the other hand, some individuals have multiple degrees and diplomas with a long list of language skills, however tend to be very shy, passive and unsure when it comes to communicating with others. This would be seen as a weakness if the person was opting to change their career into Sales. As you can see, even without specific qualifications, experience, and skills, everyone has their own strengths and weaknesses and these can be worked on constantly for one's personal and career growth.

4. Career Counselling

If you'd want some reliable assistance, career counselling would be the most recommended choice. Through interviews and tests, your appointed counselor, will determine what your strengths and weaknesses are through their standardized system and recommend positions and industries that suit your preferences and abilities.

Another option for assisting you in your quest of identifying your strengths and weaknesses is the Myers–Briggs Type Indicator (MBTI) which is a psychological-based questionnaire that identifies the different ways in which an individual thinks, acts and perceives the world around them. This report touches base on what kind of careers are best suited for a specific individual.

5. Recruitment Agency

Once you know your strengths and weaknesses, and are certain on the direction you'd like to take your career to, and you should apply to a recruitment agency. Job Agencies in Malta like Vacancy Centre recruitment will assist you with finding a job that matches your strengths and weaknesses. We keep your personal preferences in mind, as well as, regularly update you with what positions are available and what kind of salary/working conditions you may expect from certain industries. A job or vacancy centre is a specialist provider of complete recruitment solutions guaranteeing efficient and personalised Recruitment, HR Training & HR Consultancy services with maximum confidentiality. It will have an extensive network of talented candidates whose background is within the Financial, Legal & Compliance, Gaming & IT, and Administration, Sales & Marketing sectors, and has a very successful track record of delivering good talent to clients within these sectors.

Chapter 3

Use Existing Skills And Knowledge To Apply In Business Or New Careers

To be successful in your career, you need to align what you do with who you are. Sometimes, that means moving into a different field of work. But how do you move into a new industry when you've spent your professional life working in another?

Don't lose hope. You have skills, education, and training that will transfer to your new career or sector. Let's explore each of them and consider how you may be able to use them to become limitless in your career.

Transferable Skills

Which of your skills do you have that can be classed as transferable? That depends somewhat on your field and your position, but the simple answer is all of them. You can use every skill you apply in your current job in another area of work that matters to you.

Yes, you'll probably need to pick up some new skills if you want to excel in a different role. But for the most part, you'll find that you already have most of what it takes to get started. Whether your tool kit includes hard skills like management or knowledge of the law or softer skills such as empathy and organisation, transferring your skills is less about changing content and more about changing your context.

Although you may need to learn some new rules or technological points, most duties that fall under the operations, administration, and finance functions are easily transferable. Other skills, like community building and fund development, transfer well after a bit of tweaking. Selling stocks may not be the same as raising money for a nonprofit, but they both require you to do the research, ask, and follow up.

Skills that are heavily reliant on subject matter expertise are much more challenging to transfer, but this is still not an impossible route. For example, a marketing director focused on selling to educational outfits may be able to bring a quiver full of both functional and subject-matter arrows to a job raising money for a charter school association.

Formal Education

If you don't have a great deal of work experience, your formal education determines what—substantively speaking—you are qualified to do. This is critical if you're a recent graduate or don't have a long working history under your belt.

If you've been in the working world a bit longer, education is only one part of the equation. In some cases, like medicine or the law, a formal degree is a requirement. Social workers and teachers must be licensed, and stock traders and accountants must pass specific exams. In other cases, like fundraising or association management, a degree or certificate is not a requirement, but it can give you a leg up against other candidates.

In some roles, in-depth, substantive knowledge of the field is vital to a candidate's success. This is often borne out by a long career.

Medicine, for example, requires many years of training. It might not make sense to start medical school when you're 45, although this has certainly been done before.

In other cases, degrees that teach skills and not subject matter expertise—like nonprofit management, fundraising, accounting, and operations—are easily attainable and make sense strategically. It's merely a matter of determining whether the investment will deliver the returns you seek.

On-The-Job Training

Many job seekers have received enough on-the-job training to write a doctoral thesis on the work they do. Even if this is true in your working life, you probably don't realize how much you've learned along the way. You need to think about where you came from, your goals, and your career trajectory to figure out how much expertise you've acquired. The following questions might also be helpful:

- What did you hope to get from your career? Are you there?

- What changed along the way?

- What do you do now that you never imagined you would be doing?

- What do you know more about now than when you started this job/career?

As you take a deep dive into your memory, don't forget about the community service, nonprofit volunteering, or board work that you've performed. Each of your days has brought a lesson, and every experience is valuable to your job search in some way.

Sharing knowledge across your business

It's essential to avoid important knowledge or skills being held by only a few people, because if they leave or retire that expertise could be lost to your business. If you have efficient ways of sharing knowledge across the business, it will be more widely used, and its value and effectiveness are likely to be maximised.

Knowledge sharing

Consider the best ways of sharing new ideas and information with your staff. You may already have regular meetings when you can brief employees and ask them to share ideas and best practice or improvements and suggestions. A few companies in the city on London have already started to implement this process, not only does it help employees in finding that they have a voice and a say in their current positions, it also helps the company to retain valuable employees and contribute various ideas to the company policies.

One thing that could be considered is holding innovation workshops or brainstorming sessions at which staff are given the freedom and encouragement to think of ways in which the business could improve.

It can also be a good idea to create a knowledge bank containing useful information and instructions on how to carry out key tasks, mannuals or regular training sessions. Putting this on an intranet is ideal as it will encourage staff to post news or suggestions.

Knowledge management

Technology alone isn't the answer to sharing knowledge - it has to be managed carefully so that information is channelled properly. You may decide to appoint a senior manager as knowledge champion for your business.

Incentives and training

Remember that offering staff incentives to come up with suggestions for how the business can be improved is often an effective way of getting them to use and share knowledge.

Don't forget the importance of training in spreading key knowledge, skills and best practice across your business.

Create a knowledge strategy for you or your business

If you want to get the most from your business' knowledge, you need to take a strategic approach to discovering, collating and sharing it. This is done via a knowledge strategy - a set of written guidelines to be applied across the business.

If your strategy is to be effective, you must make sure your senior managers are committed to it and are fully aware of the benefits it can bring — Discuss with them the best ways of collecting and using knowledge.

When you're drawing up the strategy you need to:

- Consider how active your business currently is at using its knowledge analyse your internal processes for gathering and sharing information - are there successful ways of generating ideas and do staff have a good grasp of what's happening?

- Make sure that knowledge management, acquisition and distribution is a continuing process, so that it becomes central to your business' strategy

You should also identify the value of knowledge to your business. Think of ways you could exploit your knowledge for financial gain - perhaps by gaining a larger market share, developing new products, or selling or licensing your protected intellectual property to others. Ensure this fits in with your overall business plan.

Chapter 4

How To Transition From One Career To The Next

Looking to transition to a new career? You're not alone. A growing number of people, especially millennials, are jumping into new careers. But that doesn't mean a career change isn't a difficult process, especially if you're trying to move to an industry where you don't have much, if any, experience.

You've thought about it a hundred times. Should you do it or should you not? Should you stick with what you know or take the leap towards something new.

And, you've decided: it's finally time for a change, and not just a new job at a better company, but a whole new career in an entirely different industry.

So, now that the decision is final and you've set your eyes on the perfect role, how do you make the pivot without starting over?

How do you show employers that you have what it takes to succeed in your new industry when you technically have zero to little experience in that particular field?

So, one of the best ways to start your transition is to focus on a passion of yours.

Here are 10 important career tips that will help you discover more about yourself, allow your passions to guide you down a new career path, and help you take those first steps on your way to a new and more rewarding career.

1. Start with free association.

Take a piece of blank paper or open a blank Word document and write out everything you enjoy in life. Don't leave anything out — even things like walking the dog or cooking dinner should go on the list if you enjoy them.

Then (you guessed it), take another piece of paper or start a new document, and write out everything you don't enjoy doing. Do you see a pattern or cluster on each of these lists?

Ultimately, your ideal job will incorporate some version of the activities you enjoy while minimizing the activities you dislike. Hang onto these sheets, as they will help you along the way.

2. Be your own detective.

Research careers that incorporate activities you enjoy in life, even if they seem like a stretch at first. Read up on these careers, talk to people who are working in the field, and, if possible, tag along for a day with someone who successfully pursues the career path in which you're interested.

3. Build a vision of your life.

Based on your detective work, start to think about how your values and goals might line up with a particular career. For example, if your vision includes a more balanced lifestyle, you might have a goal of transitioning into a career that supports a healthy lifestyle while incorporating the activities you enjoy most in life.

Write your vision and goals down and keep them with your free association lists. Think of these as your planning documents - they will sustain you during your journey. After you've developed a vision for your life and researched the type of career you're interested in pursuing, it's time to look at your next steps.

4. Focus on skills and education.

If you look carefully at your work history, you'll find experience that is transferable to your new career. As you review these skills, take stock of what you need to learn in order to excel in your new career. Consider taking classes or attending conferences in your new field to refresh and build on these skills.

5. Join professional associations.

This is a great way to stay current about the trends in your potential new industry, and network with your future colleagues. In fact, professional associations quite often sponsor conferences, networking sessions, and professional development/educational opportunities for their members. In many cases, online services also will accompany your membership privileges. Take advantage of these services, as they will help keep you on track.

6. Build a relationship with a mentor.

Mentors play a unique role in your career development well beyond the transition leg of your journey. As you network, you can begin to develop several mentoring relationships. Spread yourself around, because each mentor will bring a unique perspective to your new career.

7. Try coaching to your potential.

Working with a professional career transition coach, provides a structure to your journey as well as ongoing feedback, about the choices and decisions you'll make along the way.

8. Get your foot in the door.

If possible, get involved in volunteer or part-time employment in your new field. Small opportunities build experience and provide networking and mentoring opportunities.

9. Be patient and realistic.

Patience and realistic expectations are the keys to successfully embarking on your career change. You undoubtedly will encounter obstacles and challenges along the way. Everybody does. However, if you're committed to making a career change and continue to seek assistance, your persistence will pay off.

10.   Analyze your finances.

Career change can take longer than a normal job search. For that reason, you'll need to get a handle on what you are earning and spending, and how flexible you can be. Perhaps, you can cut your expenses somewhat, allowing you the financial freedom to explore careers you had thought of, or invest in professional training for your new field.

These 10 steps show that career transition and career exploration are not like speeding down a superhighway to success.

Rather than a straight path from Career A to Career B to Career C, career transition is more like a circuitous road with peaks and valleys located along the way. However, if you follow these steps, you are likely to find the right route for you on your road to a successful career transition and rewarding new opportunities.

Chapter 5

Working As A Woman In Male Dominated Industries

Theme cluster: Unique challenges women face in male-dominated occupations

1. Formal and covert organisational practices that maintain discrimination and bias:

- Inadequate resources, biased infrastructure and policies.
- Spill over of stereotypical gender roles and expectations that relate to women.
- Lack of real transformation because of male resistance and prejudices.

2. Woman's unique physical, work identity and work-life balance needs:

- Physical and health related difficulties women experience.
- Negative work-identity perceptions.
- Work-life balance.

Theme cluster: Elements of women's resilience in male-dominated occupations

1. Coping strategies and resources:

- Appreciation of feminine advantage
- Adopting male characteristics
- Mentorship.

2. Motivational aspects of the work:

- Optimistic expectation of future career possibilities
- Challenging work and work engagement
- Recognition and success.

A description of the themes follows and gives me the understanding of the participants' experiences as women who work in male-dominated occupations.

Unique challenges that women face in male-dominated occupations

The unique challenges that emerged from the data were twofold. Firstly, the male-dominated environment seems to maintain the gender-segregated status quo formally and covertly. Secondly, the authors found that women have unique physical, work identity and work-life balance needs that challenge their ability to function easily in a male-dominated environment.

Formal and covert organizational practices that maintain discrimination and bias

Inadequate resources, biased infrastructure, and policies:

None of the participants was aware of any pertinent policies or practices that aimed to improve their integration and accommodation in the workplace.

Spill over of stereotypical gender roles and expectations that relate to women:

It was clear that the traditional gender roles and stereotypes of women in society existed in the workplace. The idea of women defying traditional cultural norms and entering gender atypical roles remained a novelty to participants' families as well as colleagues. This resulted in a lack of social, emotional and work support.

Lack of real transformation because of male resistance and prejudices:

Despite, the apparent organizational efforts to accommodate women, by employing them, in practice the women in this study experienced little genuine accommodation. Instead, they experienced vindictive and unsupportive behaviour from male colleagues. Of the women in this study, it seemed to affect those in the mining sector predominantly.

Women's unique physical, identity and work-life balance needs

Physical and health-related difficulties women experience:

- **Labour-intensive work perceptions:**
  Inadequate physical strength and hormone cycles add to the emotional strain of working in a male-dominated occupation.

- **Negative work-identity perceptions:**
  Overt and subtle practices show a prevailing lack of confidence in women's competence and their exacerbated negative self perceptions, low self-efficacy, and low self-esteem. Although none of the women in the study intended to leave their male-dominated occupations, they demonstrated a reluctance to progress into the more intensely competitive male roles because of these negative self-perceptions. Rather, they opted for those 'softer' roles whilst remaining in male-dominated environments.

- **Work-life balance:**
  The participants' different roles emerged as a source of conflict because they regularly needed to balance being primary caregivers with being career women.

Even without children and being unmarried, participants still emphasized how their prominent role in the household tax their work commitments and vice versa.

Elements of resilience for women in male dominated occupations

- **Mentorship:**
  Participants saw mentorship as a legitimate means of gaining support and guidance in the organization and of achieving career success.

Motivational work aspects

Elements of resilience that emerged from the data as relevant to motivational work aspects include:

- Optimistic career expectations
- Work engagement
- Successful career experiences.

Women In Construction

Construction is an industry that comes across and increasingly male dominated. However, there is now a slow increase in women joining the construction industrury. On average there are about 300,000 women in the UK within the construction industry, this only amount to about 4% of the population of woman. There are many benefits to why women should consider a career in construction, including:

Leadership Opportunities

The shortage of female leaders provides opportunities for women to improve team performance, contribute fresh perspectives, and advance their careers and have room for growth.

Higher Income Potential

On average, women who work construction and trade careers earn up to 30% more than traditional female-dominated careers like administrative assistants and childcare.

There is a Labour Shortage

In the next five years, the need for construction workers is expected to grow to over 1.6 million people. This opens up the opportunity for high-paying, stable jobs for women.

Feeling of Achievement

One of the best feelings is able to build something from the ground up. Working in construction allows women to receive this feeling of achievement and develop a passion for building — a passion that shouldn't be limited to just men.

Practical Skills

Construction skills like team building, managing a complex project, and working with technology and tools can be applied to other sectors and careers as well.

Sexual Harassment Is More Prevalent in Male-Dominated Industries

In a 2017 survey, 62% of the women interviewed who work in male-dominated industries in the United States reported that sexual harassment is a problem in their industry, compared to 46% of women working in female-dominated industries.

49% of women in male-dominated industries said sexual harassment is a problem in their workplaces, compared to 32% of women whose workplaces had more women than men.

28% of women working in male-dominated industries said they had personally experienced sexual harassment, compared to 20% of women in other industries.

This heightened level of harassment is a problem even before women enter the workforce. One study found that women pursuing male-dominated university majors experience higher levels of harassment than women earning other degrees. About

14% of women with engineering degrees don't enter the labor force.

Why Increased Female Interest and Participation in the Male-dominated Trades Matters?

Gender segregation of the trades matters to industry, the economy and women. Low female workforce participation rates, and the segregation of women into existing female-dominated industries contributes to labour market rigidity, suboptimal productivity, and economic inefficiency due to the lack of utilisation of the skills of women, and increased labour costs due to skills shortages. The benefits that could accrue from increased representation of women in male dominated industries are stated as:

- Accessing the talent of highly educated and skilled labour already should help lift aggregate productivity, contain wage growth, assist in lowering the future strains on the pension system and importantly help engender a more diverse workplace and a fairer society.

Women's choices, resources, and biases against them are affecting their career preferences. Many who do work in male-dominated careers face challenges of lack of support, voice, and acknowledgement of their balance between home life and their careers. The women, in turn, can create connections through affinity groups to gain support and collaboration.

There are various actions companies can take to reduce women's feelings of inequality. One example is to let women manage their own schedules, which can facilitate women's balancing act between work and home. Companies can be more proactive to create a system in which women properly are comfortable and valued in their male-dominated careers. By incorporating some of these measures, women will feel more balanced with their male counterparts in the workplace, thus helping them be more productive to the company, creating a more satisfying and successful workplace experience for all employees.

Chapter 6

Breaking Through Barriers Of Sterotypes

Productivity barriers are something that all businesses deal with at some point or another and the construction industry is no exception. Whether its higher costs, additional risks, or lack of innovation, productivity barriers can have devastating effects on business efficiency or construction. Let's look into the sterotypes within construction.

So, what are these barriers and what can we do to overcome them?

Availability of Skilled Workforce

As the baby boomer generation begins to retire, so does the construction forces most skilled workers. With so many construction workers beginning to retire, the workforce is dwindling with little enthusiasm from the younger generations. Many find it's hard to find reliable and qualified people with experience in this industry.

73

Construction jobs are no longer seen as a desirable career, and the construction industry is struggling to overcome this barrier. While this may seem like a detrimental issue, technology can help to overcome it. With new construction software applications and technological advances in construction equipment, the lack of a skilled workforce can be overcome.

50 years ago, technology was not readily available at everyone's fingertips. Today it is! Instead of wasting your time looking for the perfect skilled craftsman, use technology to train and help your workforce. In regards to people's perception of the construction industry as an undesirable profession, change the conversation. Educate the younger generations about the cutting edge technology now being used in the construction industry. Stereotypes and misconceptions are meant to be challenged so take the extra effort to target the younger workforce. They are interested in technology and you can show them that the construction industry is too!

Culture and Behaviour

Culture and behaviour is a huge factor in worker's level of job satisfaction. In the construction industry, this is one area that is severely lacking. One cultural barrier that is often talked about is the construction industries lack of importance on innovation. Many people see the construction industry as outdated and stubborn to change. Although the change may be hard when you are used to a certain way of doing things, this barrier can be overcome with an open mind. As mentioned above, technology is at our fingertips which means that innovation is also at our fingertips. Be open to new ways of doing things and try to implement innovation and fresh ideas. Your workers and potential workforce will appreciate the focus on innovation.

One behavioural barrier that remains a problem is the lack of collaboration across the supply chain. The construction industry has struggled with promoting collaboration within project teams which has led to unhappy workers. The simple solution to this is to put increased emphasis on promoting teamwork. This can be implemented through daily team meetings and discussions amongst all position levels. Devoting resources to your team will not only increase satisfaction and collaboration but foster innovation as well.

Communication

Efficient communication amongst construction teams is a barrier that all businesses face on a daily basis. With so many different individuals working together, including field workers, contractors, architects, and suppliers, it's no wonder that communication is so difficult. Luckily, affordable mobile construction software, offers a quick streamlined solution to all of your communication problems. With mobile software, your team can edit and communicate through instant messaging and collaborative document sharing in real-time. This means no more time delays or chasing down personnel! Construction software makes life easier for everyone on your team while boosting your productivity at the same time.

As our world continues to change, we need to adapt and welcome the challenges that come with it. Although the new barriers may seem discouraging, they also offer an excellent opportunity for us to improve the construction industry as a whole. The prospects are endless if you embrace the change!

Be The Woman on Top

It's not easy being a woman in a man's world, especially when you're building a career in a male-dominated industry. Even with the talk of equality between the sexes, a woman still has to work doubly hard to be respected and accepted in her chosen craft. With the right attitude and a positive outlook, however, this isn't impossible to achieve at all. In fact, it'll only be a matter of time before you find yourself the woman on top.

Dress To Impress

In any high-powered industry, first impressions always last. That's why you always have to dress to impress - a philosophy that applies to both sexes.

As a woman, you want to be taken seriously. Dressing informally and without thought of your progression, won't get you the respect you want. Dressing like a man, on the other hand, won't achieve the same thing. Indeed, in order to be taken seriously and respected, you need to dress the part.

Go for smart suits and elegant dresses that will give you an air of sophistication and professionalism. Be feminine and don't be afraid to use color. However, don't be too flamboyant and overly sexy either. This advice also applies to your shoes, bags, and other accessories. Your power dressing efforts won't go unnoticed.

Speak Up

In a male-dominated industry, women make the mistake of keeping their head down and keeping a low profile on a regular basis. You do realise, however, that you have ideas, propositions, and solutions just as good as any, so don't be afraid to speak up and get yourself heard.

Contribute to meetings on a regular basis. Share your thoughts and opinions. Take the initiative to get your proposals implemented. In other words, go beyond the realm of your comfortable workload and get yourself noticed by the people who matter.

Do not, however, overdo it. Be assertive, but not aggressive. Aggression turns men off, and the men you work with are no exceptions. Of course, be sure to contribute useful stuff. Don't just speak out for the sake of doing so, or you'll only end up embarrassing yourself. Take the initiative only when you truly have something that you feel is useful to contribute. If you are unsure, ask, this not only shows that you are willing to learn the knowledge your colleagues have, but it may also help them side with you.

Keep Your Emotions in Check

A common reason why men are wary of working with women is the fact that women are more emotional rather than rational. When you hold a high-powered career in a fast-paced industry, emotions can be a liability. Women seem to be more likely to worry in excess and lash out when emotions overtake them.

Don't succumb to feelings of rage, disappointment, or anger. If you need to cry or vent, make sure that it doesn't affect your ability to perform in the work environment. Keep your emotions in check as much as you can. Nobody wants to work with a cry-baby, and a drama queen isn't likely to be given a higher position. Emotions can take up a lot of time as a women constantly feel distracted by worry over their children, or lost in thought about other situations, they often find it harder to FOCUS on what they need to within their career to progress.

It can be helpful to take 10 minutes in the day, at any point in the day or night to check in with how you are feeling in the present moment, why you feel like that and what can be done about how you feel. Remember you have a choice on how to react to situations you come across.

Indeed, it can be difficult being a woman in a man's world. But like everything else, it's all a matter of survival. Only the fit survive, and only the fittest will succeed. You know that you do have what it takes, so don't hold back. Sooner or later, you'll find yourself the woman on top.

Chapter 7

How You Can Start Your Journey To Dominating A Male Industry

Working in a male-dominated industry comes with its own set of challenges, however, if you learn how to work with your strengths you can use those challenges and make them your strengths as a woman.

Women are marking their success in almost every professional field, but still, most of the industrial sectors are dominated by males. Gender discrimination is still prevailing in the workplace; organisations are trying to overcome it but this can't be done in a day.

In the US, 20% of software developers are women. Tech is still a notoriously sexist field: a recent study claims that "more than a third of tech industry employees have experienced or witnessed sexism."

There are cultural barriers that sometimes prevent women from being in executive roles. There is a stereotype that women can't be as good a leader as men and they can't work at higher-level positions effectively. However, we have to work together as women to fight these stereotypes by first recognizing that the problem is there and finding ways to deal with it.

Women who are employed in male-dominated industries face a variety of challenges each day such as lack of support and not having a voice. All women can, and should, make their voices heard, we can upend the gender imbalances that exist across numerous fields as women.

Know that if you are working in a male-dominated industry, you will face some challenges, but you should know how to overturn those challenges.

Here are some tips to help you start the journey and thrive in a male-dominated industry.

Be Expressive

You are confident and you have to express your ideas, thoughts, and opinions on every matter instead of being silent so that people notice you. As a woman, you can't be meek when you are in meetings with men, and you have something of value or importance to say. If you take the role of having a voice, you would get more respect in the meetings that you are apart of. Also, always be confident in your tone and let your voice be heard.

Fight Stereotypes

Women with impressive credentials do not allow stereotypes to influence them. It is, of course, a misconception that men are better at handling mentally challenging assignments than women. On the contrary, women are more often qualified to do just that with sound reasoning and better judgment, as can be better at taking the emotional responses of a client or coworker into account.

The level-headed female executive will look at male intimidation as a normal hazard at work. It is simply a defensive posture against a woman on the offensive. Maintain a professional work ethic at all times. Engage peers in sensible and enlightening discussions. Women who exude intelligence and confidence are a sight to behold. A successful woman will always be thrust in the limelight even in a male dominated industry.

Don't Get Discouraged

Career minded women can't be dissuaded from pursuing a career in a male-dominated profession. The notion that women are good only in a non-technical profession is slowly eroding. In the engineer field, for example, exceptional females are blazing their own trails.

In selected industries, the female-to-male ratio is still low and not likely to reverse in the immediate future. However, more and more women are being appointed and given the highest positions in prestigious corporations and organisations. Strong professional women possess the leadership potential to make people follow them and get things done. Female role models are emerging in every corner of the business universe.

Build Strong Relationships With Everyone

You should set a goal from the start to build a healthy relationship with your colleagues, even upper management. Your hard work, along with your strong association, will be helpful for your success within the company. At meetings or events, you should try to interact with more and more people and network. Consider that your male colleagues may be more reluctant to start a conversation or friendship with you. So, take the first step by inviting them for a drink or coffee. It will help you to make your supporters in the office.

Find a Mentor and Be a Mentor

Search for a mentor who you can trust to guide and help you. The person who inspires you and whose in a position that you aspire to be in can help save you time in reaching your goals. Listen to them and don't be afraid to ask questions and get guidance because they have been in your shoes. You should always be ready to help others. As you want a mentor so you should also be a mentor for others, especially women in your office, by supporting them so that they can succeed as well.

Don't be a pleaser

Some ladies think that by pleasing others, they will be noticed, and it will help them to get a promotion soon. It's good to be friendly with others, but remember, getting coffee for someone, or doing things outside of the scoop of your position isn't your job. Trust your skills.

Handle conflict with positivity

Instead of avoiding conflict, you should face it head-on. Communicate in a positive way that way no one feels insecure or inadequate. Communication is key to handling conflict because you need to make sure that all sides of the equation are understood. Having a great work environment that's always positive and professional can help minimize conflict. Approach problems with an attitude of problem-solving and calm.

Chapter 8

Action Plan/ Goal Setting Or Take Always

If you want to set goals, you can achieve, do not focus exessively on them. It seems that these words go against everything that is ever said about goals. A lot of people are talking about the power of setting goals but not many about how to achieve them. Yet it is a fundamental key to an all lifelong success plan.

So how can you set goals? How can you achieve them? What can you do today, tomorrow or this week that will get you closer to where you want to be?

The challenge, of course, is that we hear about setting goals so often that we tend to take it just a little bit for granted. When you get yourself to a point where you have heard it so many times, you act like you know all about it. But you need to be careful not to get caught in that trap called the law of familiarity. It is the place where you get so used to it.

The prevailing thought is to think about what you want to do. Then, you set goals, write them down, stay focused on them and go forward. You check your list over and over again, come back to it, adjust it, and that is how you achieve your goals. This is one-way people set goal, and this can work for some individuals.

Some people even do it once a year, when they make a New Year resolution. They set goals, and they do forget it until a year later. These people usually have no power. They take the goals too lightly which brings us to some basics.

You have to realize you have to practice the fundamentals daily. Think about the great coaches in sports history for example. They often teach the basics to people that are already the best at what they do. These top trainers make them go through the fundamentals over and over again, hundreds of time, day after day until they can do it at a crucial moment. Inb order to reach your goals you need to look at the type of person you need to become in order to reach your goals, also make a note of that.

Back to Basics

Should I remind you about Mr. Miyagi in "Karate Kid" with his wax on wax off? When you set goals, you have to go back and go through the basics every day. So that when you do it again, you understand how to do it even more efficiently.

If you want to reach your set goals, you have to master your skills. The reason being is that along with your journey, you make new distinctions, set new goals or even change them. So do not think for a second that you already know how to achieve them.

The bottom line often is that most people do not have a clearly defined set of objectives anyway. You need to go from the frame of mastering simple things over and over to achieve set goals. So, you have to break through the bonds of the past and look in a whole new way where you understand that you have to do whatever it takes and not be bored by basics.

Setting Goals is Powerful

Why do we need to set goals and use them? Are they important? The answer is that when you set objectives for yourself, you create the future in advance. You form your destiny and shape your life. Whether we know it or not, we all have goals.

As a result, know that your goals are affecting you. The problem is that some people have lousy goals. Those get you through the day, the week, the month or help you pay the bills but are not the kind of objectives that inspire you or make you jump out of bed in the morning. These goals do not create the drive you need to achieve something greater. Your goals need to be set in a way that possibly seem exciting and unrealistic, in order to keep your enuthisum to pursue them.

You must realise that very few people have a particular plan or even written goals. So, when you set goals, I mean real aims, you can create the power to grow, develop and expand your success. You must have something out there that is compelling enough to draw you forth and transform your life.

Reflection Time to Set Goals

Next, you have to know why you set goals, why you are doing it, and what you are moving towards. The reason being is that if you do not, you won't get the most out of yourself. You have to take time to reflect so that you can set goals. It does not matter if you reflect for days; what is important is that you do it.

Then, take two or three days to design plans and how you can achieve them. You have to set goals that are well beyond your current ability or skill. It does not matter if you have yet no idea on how to make them happen. You simply have to operate from a principle that is talked about all over the world, regardless of what you believe.

It is a common law which is the power of absolute belief and faith. If you can get inspired enough and find a goal that is exciting enough, you can figure out a way to make it happen. Even if right now it seems impossible, you can pull it off.

Set Goals in Every Area of Life

You have to set goals for yourself in every area of your life. Set them personally, emotionally, socially, physically and financially. Create an ultimate aim and what you want right now. You need objectives on who you want to be, how much happiness or passion you desire, and how you want to live every single day.

No matter the pages it could take, you should describe everything in detail, even the person of your dreams. And yes, you might create a lot of limitations or absurd goals, but if after reviewing those, your goals still make sense to you, you should believe in their realization. You have to design your own road map necessary for success.

Now you have to implement them. Of course, some of your goals will not work out, but you can achieve most of your set goals. A massive change will occur as you follow through. Your level of confidence will boost, and your faith, as well as your abilities, will change radically.

Behaviours vs. Focus for Set Goals

You need to realise that when you set goals for yourself, they are outside of your comfort zone, so if you spend too much time obessing on your goals, it can lead to none of them being achieved. By contrast, if you focus on your behaviours rather than your goals, then you can achieve your objectives.

You alone can see to your behaviors. They are what you can control. So, you have to ignore the part of your goals that you cannot influence, and focus on the part that is in your control which is behaviours. Once you focus on your actions, day after day, you begin to learn all the information you need to reach your set goals.

When you visualize your goal as already achieved, it puts you in a position where you can focus on a plan to make it. Behaviours are short term based when we set goals; it is usually seven days. So, you have to think about what you can do today, tomorrow and this week, write them down and go for it.

The Define Precision of Goals

You should act with intelligence because what real today is based on your past, on your previous experiences. So if you limit your future based on your past, you won't go anywhere. You need to set goals that are big enough to drive you. So do not stop and go "How do I do it?"

It is not the first step. The initial phase is getting it all written down, and if you do that, you can create and shape your own paradise, whatever you choose to create. It starts with a simple process of taking these generalized dream impulses and then to define them with more precision.

That is the power of goal setting. There is something beyond just what you understand of writing something down. Something happens! You become a creator when you set goals and put them down on paper. You get a clear vision while you can make them happen.

Therefore, you need to ensure that you not only set goals, but you get entirely clear why you want them. it is a fact that there is a fundamental core in goal setting that can change your life and the answer is that purpose is stronger than the outcome.

The Motivation behind Set Goals

The meaning of it is that the purpose of goals is not so you get things but rather of what they will make of you as a person. Most people set goals blindly. They desire and focus on material things. And there is nothing wrong with that; I want you to have as many things as you want because that is part of life too.

It is part of the manifestation process of creating results when you set goals. But if all you do is to focus on getting things, it may cost you your integrity of who you want to be, of what you want to create in your life. So you got to be careful!

A Final Word when You Set Goals

In conclusion, make sure that when you set a goal, you know why you are doing it. Making money motivates only so much, but becoming a person who can manifest abundance financially and physically for themselves and the people around them is rather more fulfilling. Having the freedom that money can give or have the ability to give or help others by paying it forward usually motivates more than just anything else.

So when you set goals, do not take them for granted. Focus on what you can control and let the universe take care of the rest. Do act on your intentions seriously and consistently to achieve them. I know you can go well beyond what you can dream of, I believe in you!

Conclusion

The news of the past year--with near-daily stories of sexual harassment and assault, gender inequality, and other issues affecting women in the workplace--has reinforced the fact that, however far women have come, we still live in a male-dominated world.

In a recent survey conducted by The New York Times and Morning Consult, a third of the men polled reported they had done something at work within the past year that would qualify as objectionable behaviour or sexual harassment.

We see the need for change in countries around the world and in virtually every field and industry. Good as it is that so many stories validating women's experience are coming to light, that's just the first step.

Working to bring more women into leadership is an important way to advance the cultural change we need — that means identifying prospective leaders and mentoring them through the sometimes-difficult early years of their leadership development.

It's also true that the best, most enduring change begins within, and as we're working toward cultural change we also need to work on changing ourselves--the only element we have complete control over.

We start by owning more of who we are and what we have to offer. When we do, we reclaim our power. Here are some things you can do--right now, where you are--to make it happen:

1. Become a person of value.

If you're waiting for someone to recognise the value you bring, you may well be waiting forever. Recognise your own worth. If you want to work on a project, speak up, if you want to lead a team, say so. No one would appreciate your contributions until you appreciate them yourself. Work to become known as someone who can be counted on.

2. Let your voice be heard.

Studies show women are much less likely than men to speak up in meetings--and when they do speak up, they apologize repeatedly and allow themselves to be interrupted. If you don't believe you have anything worth saying, how will others have confidence in you? Recognise the value of your opinion and believe that what you have to share is worth listening to.

3. Speak with confidence.

If your communication style seems a bit weak, practice being assertive. That doesn't mean you have to be rude or hostile. Simply drop the apologies and qualifiers when you speak and others will see you as more authoritative and confident. You will need to be convicted with what you say and in a confident and authorative way.

4. Stop trying to be a pleaser.

Many times women take on the role of the pleaser in an attempt to be noticed. If getting someone coffee isn't part of your job, let it be done by someone in an appropriate role. It's nice to be nice, but always trying to please others won't get you anywhere. Instead of serving or promoting you, it belittles you and leaves an impression that you're unsure of yourself.

5. Know your stuff and then learn some.

Play to your strengths. If you can identify what's unique in your background, use those skills to advance. And if you don't have all the skills you need to succeed, go out and learn. Take a class, read a book--do everything you can to distinguish yourself and grow professionally.

6. Learn how to handle conflict.

Instead of engaging in conflict or avoiding it, learn to communicate forward by acknowledging the conflict and asking, "So how do we move past this?" Don't make or allow personal attacks; keep it professional. Don't email when you are angry and don't read emotion or tone into texts, emails, or directives. Don't hold a grudge; once the conflict is over, shake hands, hold your head high, and get back to work.

7. Take on a leadership role.

You don't need to have a leadership title to be considered a leader in your office. Whatever your position, find a leadership role you can excel in--whether it's heading up a key initiative, solving problems and resolving conflict, or calm decision making in a crisis--and push yourself to be the go-to person for those situations.

8. Don't be afraid to ask for a raise or promotion.

When you're ready for a raise or promotion, chances are you'll be asking a male boss, and it can be intimidating. But if you've been with a company for a while and you are clearly considered a rising leader, don't be shy. Make your expectations clear and state in simple terms why they should be met. Most employers aren't going to give you a raise or the job you desire unless you request it with authority. Your boss can't argue the facts of your performance and leadership, so take the time to figure out talking points for those areas. The more data you have, the better chance you have of winning the fight.

9. Find a sponsor.

Look for sponsorship in your workplace by building strong relationships with your boss and other senior leaders. Pay particular attention to cultivating relationships with the individuals who believe in you and who publicly support you--they are going to be your best advocates and your biggest supporters.

10. Lead by example.

If every person became who they wanted to see in the world, their leadership would bridge many chasms and fill in many gaps. There's so much room for individuals to step up and out and show what true effective leadership is--and that happens through leading by example. Attract what you expect, reflect what you desire, become what you respect, and mirror what you admire.

Let's not look back but instead dream a new future by changing the present. It is time for a change, and change will come only when we as women own our own power, voices, and confidence, knowing that others will follow our lead.

Index